Following Freedom

Leni Donlan

Raintree

Chicago, Illinois

© 2007 Raintree
Published by Raintree,
A division of Reed Elsevier Inc.
Chicago, Illinois

Customer Service 888-363-4266

Visit our website at www.heinemannraintree.com

Designed by Michelle Lisseter, Kim Miracle,
and Bigtop
Printed in China

11 10 09 08 07
10 9 8 7 6 5 4 3 2 1

**Library of Congress
Cataloging-in-Publication Data**
Donlan, Leni.
  Following freedom : the Underground Railroad /
Leni Donlan.
     p. cm. -- (American history through primary
sources)
  Includes bibliographical references and index.
  ISBN 1-4109-2418-1 (hc : alk. paper) --
ISBN 1-4109-2429-7 (pb : alk.
paper)
 1. Underground railroad--Sources--Juvenile
literature. 2. Fugitive
slaves--United States--History--19th century--Sources--
Juvenile literature.
3. Antislavery movements--United States--History--
19th
century--Sources--Juvenile literature. 4. Abolitionists-
-United
States--History--19th century--Sources--Juvenile
literature. I. Title. II.
Series.
  E450.D66 2007
  973.7'115--dc22

                                        2006004014

13-digit ISBNs
978-1-4109-2418-6 (hardcover)
978-1-4109-2429-2 (paperback)

Acknowledgments
The author and publisher are grateful to the
following for permission to reproduce copyright
material: Divinity School Library, Duke University
p. 15; Elvele Images/Alamy **p. 25**; The Friends
Meeting House Collection **p. 17**; Library of Congress
Geography and Map Division **pp. 4, 6**; Library of
Congress Prints and Photographs Division **pp. 5, 7,
8, 9, 10, 11, 13, 19, 23**; Spring Hill Collection p. 17.

Cover image of "The Underground Railroad"
reproduced with permission of Library of Congress
Prints and Photographs Division.

Photo research by Tracy Cummins.
Illustrations by Darren Lingard.

The publishers would like to thank Nancy Harris and
Joy Rogers for their assistance in the preparation of
this book.

Every effort has been made to contact copyright
holders of any material reproduced in this book. Any
omissions will be rectified in subsequent printings if
notice is given to the publishers.

Disclaimer
All the Internet addresses (URLs) given in this book
were valid at the time of going to press. However, due
to the dynamic nature of the Internet, some addresses
may have changed, or sites may have changed or
ceased to exist since publication. While the author and
publishers regret any inconvenience this may cause
readers, no responsibility for any such changes can be
accepted by either the author or the publishers.

It is recommended that adults supervise children on
the Internet.

Contents

Some words are printed in bold, **like this**. You can find out what they mean on page 30. You can also look in the box at the bottom of the page where they first appear.

A Train to Freedom

The Underground Railroad did not run on tracks. It did not have engines or cars. The Underground Railroad did carry passengers, though. Those passengers were escaped **slaves**. Slaves are people who are owned by someone else.

There were slaves in America in the early 1600s. People in the United States were allowed to own slaves up until the late 1860s.

▲ This is a map of the United States. The states that had slaves are in dark and light brown.

The Underground Railroad was a secret group of people.
They worked together to help slaves escape to freedom.

Let's find out more about the Underground Railroad. What
was it? How did it come to be? *All aboard* . . .

These slaves escaped ▼
to freedom.

5

slave person owned by another person

Taken from Africa

Slaves were often taken from Africa. For over 300 years, many Africans were **kidnapped**. They were taken from their homes. Then they were taken to the United States by ship. The Africans were joined together by chains. Sadly, many died on these ships.

Olaudah Equiano lived in Africa. He was eleven years old when he was kidnapped. Years later, he remembered: *"They tied our hands … We were unable to take any food … our only relief was some sleep."*

◄ *This map shows Africa in 1688.*

6

slavery	practice of buying and selling slaves
kidnap	take someone away from a place against their will

It could take months for a slave ship to get from Africa to the United States. When the ship arrived, the Africans were sold as slaves. They could also be traded as slaves. Someone who buys or sells people for money is practicing **slavery**.

▲ Africans were crowded onto the decks of slave ships.

7

Life in Slavery

The Africans were sold at an **auction**. An auction is a public sale. Buyers called out their **bids**. The bid was the price they were willing to pay for the **slaves**. The buyer who made the highest bid owned the slave.

The slaves' owners could treat their slaves however they wished. They could make them clean and cook. They could beat their slaves. They could feed and clothe them well. They could treat them badly.

▼Buyers bid on the slaves they want to buy.

Slave families were often torn apart. Fathers, mothers, and children might be sold to different owners. The family could be apart for years.

Slave owners wanted to keep slaves from running away. They punished the slaves. It was very difficult for a slave to run away. It was also very dangerous.

◀ Fathers could be sold without their families.

auction public sale
bid   amount of money someone is willing to pay for what is on sale

Abolishing Slavery

Some people were against **slavery**. **Abolitionists** were people who wanted to stop slavery. The word *abolish* means to stop or prevent something.

Abolitionists spoke against slavery in public speeches. They tried to make laws to stop slavery. Some helped **slaves** to escape.

Abolitionists came from different backgrounds. Some had been slaves themselves. Do you recognize any of these famous abolitionists?

Harriet Beecher Stowe

▲ She wrote Uncle Tom's Cabin. *This book spoke out against slavery.*

Benjamin Franklin

▲ *He may be best remembered for his inventions. He also helped create the Declaration of Independence.*

Frederick Douglass

He escaped from slavery as a ▶ young man. He worked hard to help others to freedom. He also gave many public speeches. He spoke out about ending slavery.

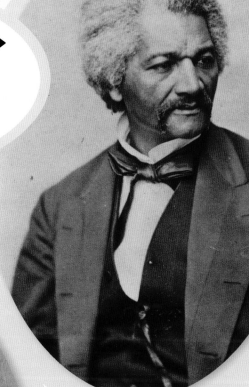

Sojourner Truth

▲ She also escaped from slavery. Then she worked for the freedom of all people.

11

abolitionist   person who was against slavery and worked to stop it

Riding the Underground Railroad

Conductors

The Underground Railroad was not a train. It was a group of people. They wanted to help people escape from **slavery**. They did not have a real train. But, like a railroad, they used a **route** (path). They helped escaped **slaves** along this route. This route led to freedom in the North.

Conductors were part of the Underground Railroad. They went into slave **territory**. Slave territory was an area where slaves lived. They guided runaway slaves to freedom.

Harriet Tubman was a conductor. She spent her childhood as a slave. She escaped from slavery when she was an adult. She escaped to the city of Philadelphia.

Tubman believed it was her right to be free. She would rather be dead than be a slave. She said:
"No man should take me alive . . . [I would] fight for my liberty [freedom] so long as my strength lasted."

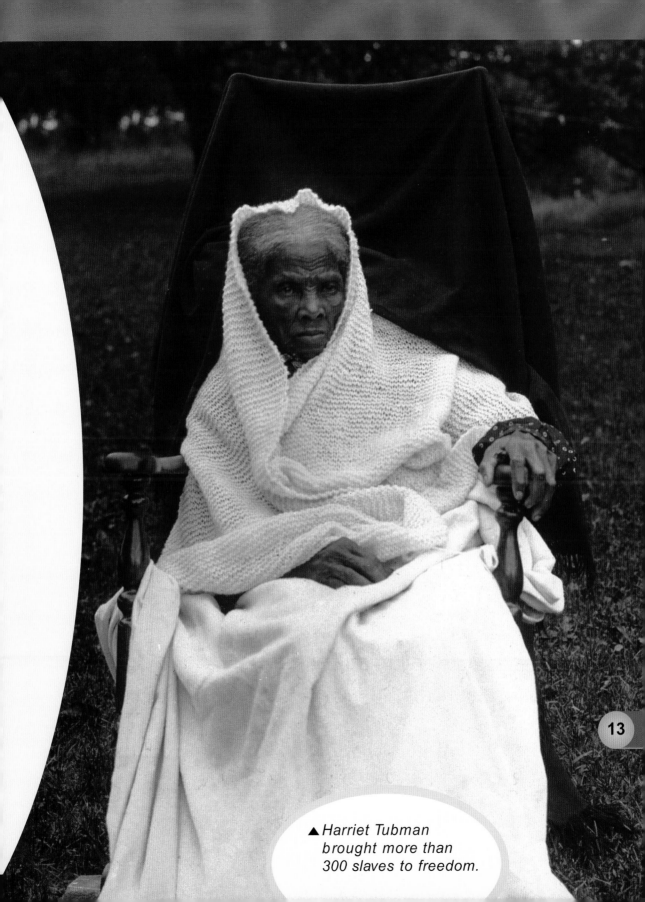

▲Harriet Tubman brought more than 300 slaves to freedom.

Leading the way

Jermain Wesley Loguen and Harriet Tubman were friends. Loguen was an escaped **slave**, too. When he was 21 years old, he ran away from his owner. He went north to Detroit, Michigan. Then he went on to Canada.

▼ *This sign advertised that $100 would be paid to a slave hunter who found and returned the missing slave.*

$100 REWARD!
RANAWAY

From the undersigned, living on Current River, about twelve miles above Doniphan, in Ripley County, Mo., on 2nd of March, 1860, A NE GROMAN about 50 years old, weighs about 160 pounds; high forehead, with a scar on it; had on brown pants and coat very much worn, and an old black wool hat; shoes size No.11.

The above reward will be given to any person who may apprehend this said negro out of the state; and fifty dollars if apprehended in this state out side of Ripley county, or $25 if taken in Ripley county.

APOS TUCKER

*Jermain Wesley Loguen was ▶ a **conductor** on the Underground Railroad. He bravely rescued many slaves.*

*Yours truly
J.W. Loguen*

Loguen went to school. He became the leader of a church. He also opened two schools for black children in New York. He wrote articles for an **abolitionist** newspaper. The newspaper printed articles that spoke against **slavery**.

Jermain Wesley Loguen helped 1,500 slaves escape to freedom. It was dangerous work. But danger did not stop him.

Escaped slaves were always in danger. **Slave hunters** were paid to find and return slaves. The slave hunters were paid a **bounty** (reward). They would grab escaped slaves. They would take the slaves back to their owners.

| **bounty** | payment or reward for catching criminals or runaway slaves |
| **slave hunter** | person who tracked down, found, and returned runaway slaves |

Stations

Escaped **slaves** headed to the closest free area. Free areas did not allow **slavery**. Northern cities were often free areas. Philadelphia, Pennsylvania, Cincinnati, Ohio, and Detroit, Michigan, were all free areas.

People on the Underground Railroad knew how to get slaves to free areas. They knew where secret hiding places were along the **route** (path) to these areas.

The Underground Railroad had **stations**. These stations were safe places for escaping slaves to hide. Sometimes stations were private homes. Sometimes stations were public buildings.

The stations were owned by **agents**. Agents were people who helped runaway slaves. They gave them food, clothing, and money. They gave them safe places to hide.

DANGER!

People caught helping an escaped slave also faced danger. They could be put in jail. They could be made to pay a fine of $500 or more.

agent   person who helped escaped slaves

station   safe place for slaves to hide while they were escaping to freedom

⬍ These two houses were used as stations by the Underground Railroad. They were used to keep slaves safe. Spring Hill in Northern Ohio (above) had a hidden staircase.

Anything for Freedom

Not all **slaves** used the Underground Railroad to escape from **slavery**. Henry Brown had a special plan of his own. He had himself shipped in a box to freedom!

Henry had the box shipped from Richmond, Virginia, to Philadelphia, Pennsylvania. Richmond was in slave **territory**. Slaves lived there. Philadelphia was a free area. There was no slavery in Philadelphia.

Henry hid in the box. The box was sent to a Pennsylvania group. The group was against slavery. They pulled Henry out of the box. They pulled him to freedom.

Freedom was not easy to get. A slave had to be brave. A slave needed to have a good plan. A slave needed help from others.

Not many slaves shipped themselves to freedom. But the risk and danger in Henry's story are not unusual.

▼Henry Brown escaped from slavery in a box.

DANGER!

Over 100,000 slaves ran away to freedom. They were willing to do anything to be free. They were even willing to risk their lives.

Signals, Songs, and Codes

Signals

How did **slaves** know when, where, and how to escape?

It is not possible to know for sure. Some people believe that **patterns** (designs) were used to send messages to slaves. The patterns were on **quilts** (blankets). It is believed that quilts were hung carefully in special places. Then slaves could read the secret messages in the quilt patterns.

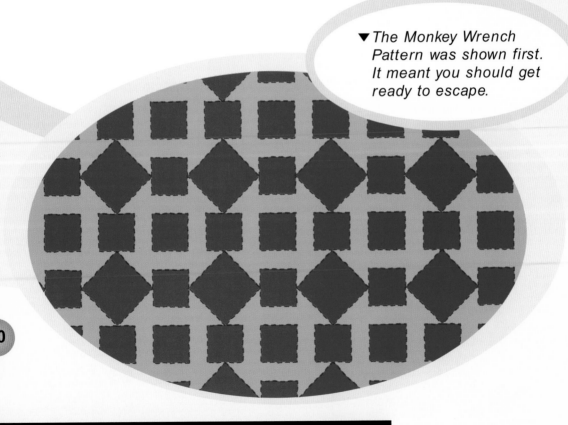

▼ The Monkey Wrench Pattern was shown first. It meant you should get ready to escape.

pattern	model for making something
quilt	blanket made of two layers of cloth that are filled with stuffing and stitched together

The Wagon Wheel Pattern ▶ was next. This pattern meant you should pack for a long journey.

Next came the Bear's ▶ Paw Pattern. When slaves saw this, they should get ready to head north. By following bear tracks, slaves could find water and food.

The Tumbling Blocks Pattern ▲ was last. This meant that a **conductor** (guide) or **agent** (helper) was in the area. The time was right for escape.

Songs

Songs were also used to share secret instructions. The song "Wade in the Water" gave **slaves** a message. The song's words told slaves to wade (walk) through rivers and streams.

Slave hunters looked for escaped slaves. They used dogs to help hunt for escaped slaves. The dogs could smell and track humans. Dogs found it difficult to track slaves if the slaves were in water. The song "Wade in the Water" warned escaped slaves about this.

FREEDOM SONGS

*Harriet Tubman often sang different songs to warn slaves. Harriet would walk where slaves could hear her singing. Slaves knew that the songs were **codes**. Codes have secret meanings. They tell messages in a different way than plain words. Harriet's songs told the slaves that she had come. She had come to lead them to freedom on the Underground Railroad.*

code   system of symbols (such as letters or numbers) that are used to share messages

▼ Moving through water could help slaves escape from slave hunters and their dogs.

IN THE SWAMP.

Codes

The song "Follow the Drinking **Gourd**" also had a message. It told escaped **slaves** to look for the North Star.

The North Star is in the Little Dipper **constellation**. A constellation is a group of stars. The stars in the Little Dipper look like a long-handled dipper (cup). They also look like a gourd. A gourd is a hard-shelled fruit. When empty, a gourd can be used as a cup.

The words of the song were used as a **code**. A code tells you how to find different meanings in information. The code told slaves to follow the constellation that looked like a drinking gourd. By following the North Star, slaves could find their way to freedom. They could head for freedom in the northern states.

Do the words of the song sound like directions for escape to you?

> The river ends between two hills
> Follow the drinking gourd.
> There's another river on the other side
> Follow the drinking gourd.
>
> Where the great big river meets the little river
> Follow the drinking gourd.
> The old man is a-waiting for to carry you to freedom
> If you follow the drinking gourd.

Can you see the ▼ dipper (cup shape) in this constellation?

North Star

Little Dipper

constellation   group of stars
gourd   hard-shelled fruit

Destinations

After months of travel, **slaves** reached their **destination**. A destination is the place a person is trying to get to. Many escaped slaves went to northern cities. Other slaves stayed with Native American tribes.

Years later, these escaped slaves were still living in North Carolina and Louisiana. Some stayed in the mountains of Tennessee and Kentucky. Other slaves went to Canada, Mexico, or the Caribbean nations.

There is a story told about one escaping slave. This slave reached the Ohio River. His owner was very close to catching him. The slave swam across the river as fast as he could. His owner followed him in a boat. Somehow, the slave reached land first. Then he disappeared!

The slave owner searched long and hard. Then he gave up the search. He said his slave had "gone off on an underground railroad."

That slave owner was right!

destination place that a person is trying to get to

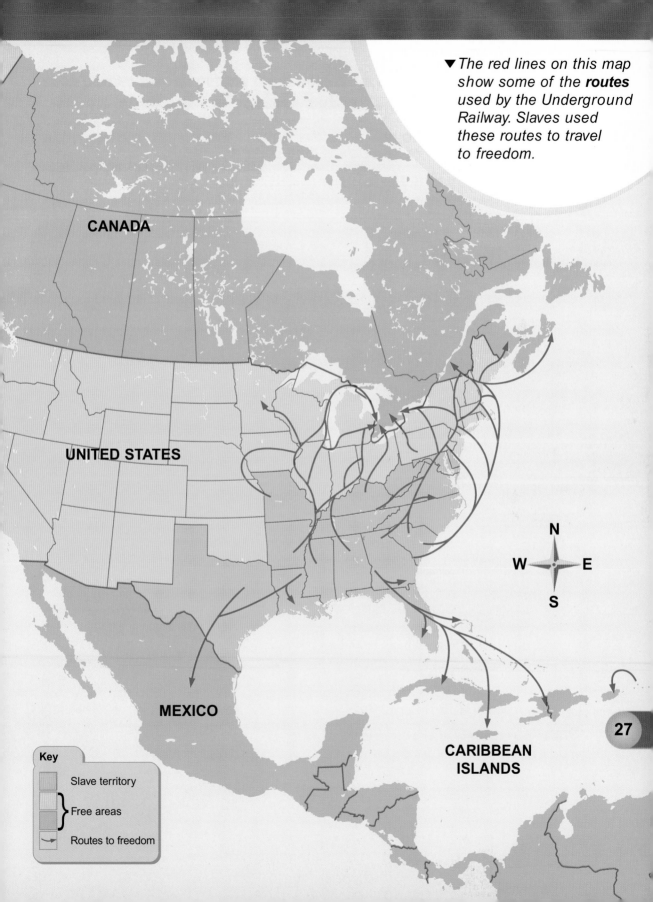

▼ The red lines on this map show some of the **routes** used by the Underground Railway. Slaves used these routes to travel to freedom.

CANADA

UNITED STATES

MEXICO

CARIBBEAN ISLANDS

N
W   E
S

Key
Slave territory
Free areas
Routes to freedom

Stations on the Underground Railroad

Stations (safe places) existed in many homes and buildings. They were along the **routes** (paths) of the Underground Railroad.

1 Milton House in Wisconsin

Slaves entered through the log cabin. They walked through a tunnel to the basement. Joseph Goodrich and his family gave them food and a place to stay.

2 Spring Hill Home in Ohio

Thomas and Charity Rotch's home was a station on the Underground Railroad. They hid runaway slaves well. No slave was ever caught at Spring Hill.

3 White Horse Farm in Pennsylvania

White Horse Farm was the home of Elija Pennypacker. It became a stop on the Underground Railroad in 1840.

4 Friends Meeting House in Delaware

The Friends Meeting was in Wilmington, Delaware. It was the last stop before freedom for many escaping slaves.

Glossary

abolitionist person who was against slavery and worked to stop it

agent person who helped escaped slaves. Agents gave slaves food, clothing, money, and safe places to hide.

auction public sale

bid amount of money someone is willing to pay for what is on sale. Also, when a person calls out how much he or she is willing to pay.

bounty payment or reward for catching criminals or runaway slaves

code system of symbols (such as letters or numbers) used to share messages

conductor person who collected runaway slaves and guided them to freedom

constellation group of stars

destination place that a person is trying to get to

gourd hard-shelled fruit. When empty, it can be used as a cup.

kidnap take someone away from a place against their will

pattern model for making something

quilt blanket made of two layers of cloth that are filled with stuffing and stitched together

route path that is traveled

slave person owned by another person

slave hunter person who tracked down, found, and returned runaway slaves

slavery practice of buying and selling slaves

station safe place for slaves to hide while they were escaping to freedom

territory special area of land

Want to Know More?

Books to read

- Hamilton, Virginia. *Many Thousand Gone: African Americans from Slavery to Freedom*. New York: Knopf, 1993.
- Levine, Ellen. *If You Traveled on the Underground Railroad*. New York: Scholastic, 1993.
- McDonough, Yona Zeldis. *Who Was Harriet Tubman?* New York: Grosset & Dunlap, 2002.

Websites

- http://nasaexplores.nasa.gov/extras /constellations/follow_the_drinking_ gourd_07-03-03.html

This National Aeronautics and Space Administration (NASA) site has the complete lyrics and a sound file of "Follow the Drinking Gourd." Crack the song's code!

- http://www.americaslibrary.gov/ cgi-bin/page.cgi/aa/activists/tubman This Library of Congress site shares stories about the life and work of Harriet Tubman.
- http://www.americaslibrary.gov/cgi-bin/page.cgi/aa/activists/douglass This Library of Congress site shares stories about the life and work of Frederick Douglass.

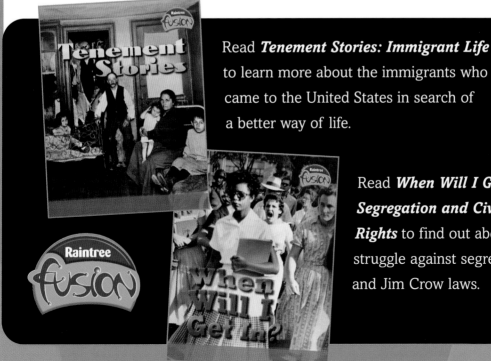

Read *Tenement Stories: Immigrant Life* to learn more about the immigrants who came to the United States in search of a better way of life.

Read *When Will I Get In?: Segregation and Civil Rights* to find out about the struggle against segregation and Jim Crow laws.

Index